I0096757

SPIN INFINITY

Praise for *Spin Infinity*

"In Lynn Rather's remarkable book of poems called Spin Infinity one is reminded on every page of the shocking power of poetry to console, to heal, and to name the very interstices of our precarious human position on earth as she herself 'fell up into a kind of Grace/and all was Beloved.' And somehow we as readers, through her wise and quiet words, are also lifted and cherished and made holy and whole once more. Indeed, this book is a pure and rare reminder of how truly precious it simply is to be. An astonishment."

-Robert Vivian, author of *All I Feel Is Rivers*

"Every time I read Lynn's words I feel that I am fulfilling Rumi's command to 'open the window in the center of your chest, and let the spirits fly in and out.' In her words everything that is mundane becomes divine; everything intimate becomes cosmic. Each line launches into the universe and lands on the rose petal. In her mention of a geese and flowers we find the spinning of the stars. With every reading my spirit flies, and my soul is nurtured. She has become part of my daily devotional reading."

-Michelle Lucchesi, MA Psychologist, Rumi Hour poet, Artistic Director of My Turn Performing Arts Collective

"Lynn Rather has written a collection of exercises in being. Being with the divine, being with the mundane, being with yourself, because there really is no difference. Carl Jung said 'people don't find God, because they don't look low enough.' Lynn has figured out how to look low enough. In documenting a life of finding God in the spaces between sentences and and the spaces between stars, she's given us something to help us look low enough too."

-Kathryn Zettel, Rumi Hour poet

SPIN INFINITY

Poems

LYNN RATHER

IF Press

Spin Infinity
Copyright © 2023 Lynn Rather
ISBN: 979-8-218-12812-8
All rights reserved.

First paperback edition March 2023
IF Press
314 Pleasant Ave
Alma, MI 48801
Cover and text designed by Joshua Zeitler

.

CONTENTS

ACKNOWLEDGMENTS

To the Rumi Hour poets

with special thanks to Joshua Zeitler for his
tireless work in bringing this book to fruition.

In gratitude for his vision.

FOREWORD

You, reader, are holding something precious.

Something like a soft pebble, with a planetary arc and gravity.

When I first met Lynn Rather, we were both janitors in Alma College's main academic building, SAC. Most of the time I saw her in passing—she was arriving for second shift and I was leaving first. We'd linger with the floor buffers in the loading bay outside the break room and exchange small talk and gossip before the official changing of the guard. She had a deep, raspy voice with a leisurely cadence and a grizzled, no-bullshit attitude. Our relationship quickly surpassed acquaintances, falling perhaps just short of friends.

Still, I hadn't suspected at the time that she was such an avid reader, much less writer, of poetry. Then our paths crossed again years later at the Rumi Hour, a leaderless poetry group that meets in a locally-owned coffee shop in downtown Alma every Thursday afternoon. When I started attending, I was recovering from my latest psychiatric hospitalization and turning once again to poetry in a restless search for meaning. I would share new poetry when it came to me, but more often I'd just read the latest epiphany Jane Hirshfield had given me. It's the kind of group we are: faithful lovers who have carved out a time where words are sacred. Creativity encouraged, not required. Share what moves you.

The first time Lynn shared a poem she had written, she made little fanfare, and I remember being under the impression that it was in fact the work of W. S. Merwin. I must have asked to clarify who had written it so I could look into their bibliography, and when Lynn responded that she had, I was pleasantly surprised.

The times she shared her own work were sometimes few and far between—Lynn admits that she can go long periods of time without reaching the page—but each time she did, it made a distinct impression on me. It became something I looked forward to. Lynn's words, especially in her voice, carry a mystic wisdom not unlike Mary Oliver's, or my beloved Jane Hirshfield's. Whenever I was thrashing wildly about for meaning, they calmed me, reminded me of the stilled center.

So when I got it into my head that I was going to learn bookbinding as a physical activity to help center myself, I immediately thought of Lynn. I was nervous at first to ask her permission to print her work. It was no small measure of trust I was asking her to place in me, but I knew that I wanted to create something meaningful, something precious. To my relief, Lynn said yes.

It has been an immense honor to shepherd her precious poetry into the book you now hold. I have tried to interfere as little as possible. We began working from a stuffed folder—I had her type and print for me every poem that felt complete to her. I read the poems, spread them out on the floor, listened, let the resonances between them suggest orders, divisions, the titles of sections and the collection.

The first printing of this book was a run of 11 copies. The text was printed on cream paper in three signatures, which I folded and sewed together by hand. The covers were cut from chipboard and wrapped in lilac cloth. They were, I hope, as beautiful a container as the contents.

It wasn't long, however, before the demand for Lynn's poetry outstripped my ability to make them. I hope that this new form allows her words to find their way into the hands of anyone who needs them—and I do believe wholeheartedly that the world needs them.

Lynn's work radiates hope, but it is a hope that is hard-won. Her awe and gratitude are not wild fruits, but carefully cultivated skills. And I hope that you, whoever and wherever you are, find in them that "sliver of light / pulling you toward dawn."

-Joshua Zeitler

O body swayed to music, O brightening glance,
How can we know the dancer from the dance?

—William Butler Yeats

Life, so-called, is a short episode
between two great mysteries...

—Carl Jung

Human beings, vegetables, or
cosmic dust, we all dance to a
mysterious tune, intoned in the
distance by an invisible piper.

—Albert Einstein

I

UTTERLY

The Old Farmhouse

the old farmhouse stood tall and alone,
as in a white frock dress,
her bushes neat, and trimmed,
seas of corn rustling around her.

upstairs, the dark cavern of rooms
with worrying cracks in the ceiling,
and yellowed shades, drowsy eyelids
drawn against the morning bright and birdsong.

at night, from the crossroad tavern,
a Blatz beer sign blazed
across the fields, and farmers drank drafts
before riding the dark roads home.

Dad at 89

Asleep sitting up,
your back bent nearly double
bones bent like a corncrib under snow,

over old snapshots you perk up,
bits of memory surface
and ripple out like rows of corn.
the farmhouse and field,
people long gone, mute and unmoving,
staring out from flat pages.
you know all their stories,
the plow horses before the tractor,
girlfriends leaning against an old Ford,
Uncle Nabert before the war,
an entire lifetime trailing behind you,
a road disappearing into the horizon.

you seem to shine inside
your own life now;
at once, a little boy beside a barn,
and an old man brushing crumbs
from his face.

Soft Places

there is a softness, an entering,
when I remember my mother's smell.
I see green kitchen tiles in sunlight,
and hear her humming,
which goes on without her
in that Illinois air above
the house no longer there.

my father, with his weary work,
always work, and gray work clothes
smelling of metal pipes and dust,
and the damp, rocky crawl space,
his hands too big for little girls.
I will not know his soft places
for sixty-five years.

In the House of Hours

sleepless at 3 a.m., silence.
cigarette smoke curls around a lamp,
a purring cat keeps vigil.

outside the snow falls gently,
there are sounds of a jet faraway,
stars arc overhead in crisp, frozen distance.

what am I searching for?
what space within longs to be filled?
how can the stars not be enough?

Milky Way

no two snowflakes alike,
nor galaxies, nor mothers.
an aroma of Christmas cookies
hangs in the air—snickerdoodle,
spritz, rosettes, butter cookies,
you sit dozing on the sofa
with Mitch Miller on tv.

sometimes you go away,
down some river of memory, or thought,
in a boat by yourself,
as invisible path runs back
over our lives, leading to now,
and the Milky Way floats above.

Reflection

the Universe has no center or edge.
it's the same with us,
rowing toward an illusion
of shore,
all the while knowing
we are both rower, and shore,
faint stars blinking
their million mile distance,
our reflection smiling
in a ring of water,
one circle among many.

A God Humming

Vocatus atque non vocatus Deus aderit
"Bidden or not bidden, God is present"

everything changes, something shifts...
rising, falling, opening, closing,
some moments in our lives arrive so softly
they go unnoticed.
God enters our knowing
through a secret gate, beckoning, inviting.
    God in a spiderweb, glistening with dew,
    God in a baby's hand, God in a dog's eye,
    God in the refrigerator humming.
for so long in my life,
I could not imagine Her presence within me,
growing like a strange fetus,
pregnant with possibilities,
when did the closing begin, the shutting down?
I felt underwater and far away.
no matter. I have let go the God of my youth.
it was someone else's idea of God.
    God in a sleeping cat, curled in a patch of sun,

God in a teabag, God in an acorn,
God in the produce section,
God arriving at Gate 7.
they say He works in mysterious ways,
but he is also clear and plain,
simple as an empty bowl,
sensible as a good pair of shoes,
palpable as oatmeal;
circles ripple out from stones dropped in water.
God at the front door, ringing the bell,
God in the laundromat, in the rinse cycle,
God in the details, God in the vast,
God in the spinning wheels of trucks and
   chakras.
O God of Everything, luminous One,
in my deepest darkness you were there,
ringing like a bell in the distance.
She who gives birth, She who weaves patterns,
She who draws us toward
the cauldron of changes—
all life whirling and buzzing with the holiness of
   itself,
dragonflies, drunks, and snow-covered spruce trees.
God within and around us—
God who dances and delights and weeps,

God who sings little songs to children and
    animals—
May your Presence grow
into my small understanding.

Once

Once,
when I was underground
I felt the world's dark pulse,
and roots and tendrils, pebbled seams
sang their being into place,
and the earth dreamed.
I must honor the deep space within.

once
when I was undersea
I heard her weighted water
shifting and turning in the night.
Beneath belled buoys I fell,
I heard stories only water can tell.
I must love my darkness back up to light.

What Remains

for KyAnne

fog shrouds everything
this morning
I am thinking of you

gone from us at last.
what is given
returns to its source.

what is taken away
remains somehow,
your absence so present,

like an empty cup,
or a room
with many windows.

Unscathed

keep going.
just keep going, in a straight line,
no zigging, no zagging.

pull a string,
and a light comes on,
darkness recedes.

push a button,
and the bottom falls out.
you fall up, into starlight,
and keep going.

The Way Home

"What empties itself falls into the place that is open."
            Jane Hirshfield

sometimes death comes so quickly, quietly,
  so unexpectedly,
like a dory loosened from its moorings,
  gliding silently away on mirrored water.

how can we speak of eternity?
  of a moment?
    a door opens—
    a dewdrop falls from a leaf—
    a string of lamps lights the avenue—

what shall be our compass,
  our true north of the soul,
    when our eyes explode in light?
    a bell tolls in the distance—
    moonlight floods the sleeping earth—
    geese fly overhead—

and yet we do know the way home.
  we always have,
as surely as the yearning of space to fill itself,
  and overflow, and empty again.

   we breathe in and out—
   a breeze blows the curtain in an open window—
   the soft fluttering of wings—

sometimes it is so much,
  it is enough, it is All,
    just to be here, to be utterly present.

Memo to Self

stop thinking so much.
you look for divinity everywhere
but inside yourself.

just to be is holy.
note the little breeze
and the wrens.

How to Be Still

focus on geese honking overhead,
taking deep breaths.
turn off the tv, burrow into silence
'til you hear your own molecules spinning.
try to nail moonlight to a wall,
or count the dots in the ceiling tile.
close your eyes, drift beyond
the known circle of things;
on one side is everything you are,
step slowly away.

The Drifting

furiously the wind howls,
driving snow and debris before it.

gusts scream eerily through cracks.
pictures shudder on walls.

on nights like this I think
I have not loved enough,
I have not given as much as I could.

snow blows and drifts across fields.
that is what it does.

the wind roars and then is gone.
that is what it does.

they give themselves utterly, and move on.

2

TOWARD DAWN

hurry
  auto again
same wheels grinding county after county
    in new mud.
The drunken eyes in the front seat
  are waiting for nothing,
taking in miles blankly
  as each rolls beneath.
in two days Oklahoma!

chug clunk
  the motor music
Volkswagen beams eyeing
the stretch of earth before us.
  imagine
what lies between here and destination
    to be spoken or done,
future strung state to state
  like telephone poles.

all the world's a driving wheel
across time and distance
there's no turning back
we shrink and expand
wander to come home

in another time I was that boy
hearing a locomotive whistle
its distance, getting closer and closer,
imagining faraway places, wild places,
places past the rim
of my understanding

what is the weight
of a nine-year-old's dreams
across time and space
there's no turning back

your death now
a calm, still lake
between here and gone.

your blue, blue eyes,
the Nelson nose, Chanel no. 5.
I still feel the touch of your hand
unlike any other.

so many jumping off points.
our lives fill and empty and fill
until all that is unnecessary
falls away,
blown to some new belonging.

you are disappearing,
there, but not there
like an unmarked road passed by
in the dark, unnoticed.
childhood long gone,
the house gone too.
no bread crumbs to mark
a path back, only forward,
a sliver of light
pulling you toward dawn.

the way fall light
makes the old dresser glow
reminds me of the Civil War
and a sparse farmhouse bedroom
soft and grey
a dresser waits for someone
who will not return
whispers of other lifetimes
houses, furniture as witnesses
light as memory

cold, grey drizzle
geese flying south
calling for change

moods like clouds
rain patter on porch chairs
I listen for hours, comforted

I am cleansing my body
of a darkness not mine to hold,
I go on listening to rain.

depressed, crabby, moody,
chores piling up, worry wasting,
watching WW2 in color.
wind roars outside.
I want oblivion.
I want a deeper place to be,
I want to grow into the rest
of my life with abandon.
I want an opening to fly through.
This is why I listen to the birds.

I am a black hole falling into myself

I am a dream I had when I was 7

I am who I am and not
who I wanted to be

I am anti-depressants and feeling like
the color beige

I am what the trees said
when I wasn't listening

I am in the space between sentences
where God also resides

I am the field of sugar beets you're driving by
I am also what the bean field is not

I am disappearing down a road
rimmed with chicory and Queen Anne's lace

I am here and not here, everywhere
and nowhere at the same time

I am the dance of Shiva
and a flock of starlings lifting off

That humming sound
is just the world turning

what does it mean to be here
  walking across the earth?
as my 64-year-old self drives north
  farms and furrowed fields float past.
I am alive in the world, alive in the world,
  breathing in, breathing out,
learning to let in and let go.

O God of All That Is
let judgment fall away,
  let my need for certainty fade.
I wonder at how the world
  keeps turning.
O for the Silent Center,
  let's just dance, let's just dance...

a pack of blue papers says
sick of the old,
not sure where new is.
replaying old scenes,
old thoughts that lead nowhere
except back to the cycle.
a new play is trying to be written.
even my dreams are changing.
I want to paint my front door purple.

it's an inch apart,
the distance between
a wisp of spirit and weightlessness

between the beating heart
of a vole under snow
and a flutter of wings

between a mouthful of sand
and all the burning words
I never wrote or spoke

between the last breath
and the Light
that surpasses all

3

ETERNITY AROUND US

eternity around us
in a Walmart parking lot.
snow squalls swirl,
people huddle and hurry.

wheels spinning on ice,
worlds spinning around us.
I go in for litter,
come out to white wonder.

all that remains is silence
and tire tracks in snow

I am a pilgrim walking in circles
toward a door
to everything as it is—

clouds roll by a Beaver moon,
the maples, the crickets and birdsong
all say HERE, NOW
all paths lead nowhere

act like you belong here.
act like you have a voice
and something to say
and the courage to say it!
your vision of how to be in this world
and what that means matters.

why are you so sad?
afraid to join the noisy world,
to participate.
it's all waiting for you
to open into it.
you're not separate.
rub up against the world,
step into it,
your destination is you.

it was something I didn't know I knew
everything was the same but different
and there was a sound that was
not a sound
more like a filling up
and everything hummed
and glowed from inside
I fell up into a kind of Grace
and all was Beloved
and all things became new
anything unresolved fell away
and all I felt was stars

"Earth's crammed with heaven"
        Elizabeth Barrett Browning

stunning clouds,
a summer storm has passed,
sun pokes out in the west,
everything green and dripping,
all grateful for the long drink.
I felt I was in Heaven,
a Heaven of sorts, and I wept.
Paradise all around us
beaming with merely being.

one July
when the fireflies were out
and a mist rose from the fields

I felt a pulsing hum and buzz
and understood my longing
to connect with something real

like my mother's face
or the light
behind your eyes

two blue flies on the porch rail,
iridescent, happily abuzz

I envy their simplicity
not needing
answers or meaning or religion

meanwhile
our magnificent little lives
take place

atoms and chakra and clocks
spinning here
stars and galaxies spin above
two blue flies on the porch rail

it was the music
that told the story

how a melody runs through everything
no louder than bees' wings

how the thread of things
runs through a lifetime

and you see how it all was and why
how the seasons fold into each other

meanwhile the asters
and rose of Sharon purple the air

as the music of spheres
sings my bones into words

it's so big
where we belong
remember running as a child
what the wind said
as it raced by your ears
how your body felt
you owned it
you owned that space
your body moved easily
everything flowed
toward something
the startling hereness of Here

what if I told you
it shines inside everything

there's no secret to living
every day is enough
ask the tree frogs, the foxglove
what they need to understand

across the world
bar-headed geese fly over
the Himalayas
a woman washes her clothes in a river
a pathway disappears

across the universe
of black holes and bumblebees
we spin in an infinity
disguised as daily life

ABOUT THE AUTHOR

LYNN RATHER lives in Michigan with her cats, rocks and fossils, perennial gardens, and a great love for poetry.

www.ingramcontent.com/pod-product-compliance
Lightning Source LLC
Chambersburg PA
CBHW060257030426
42335CB00014B/1749

* 9 7 9 8 2 1 8 1 2 8 1 2 8 *